Level 4

Sleeping Beauty

Retold by Sue Arengo
Illustrated by Jérôme Brasseur

❧ Contents ❧

OXFORD
UNIVERSITY PRESS

Once upon a time there was a king and queen. They lived in a big castle. They did not have any children, but they wanted a child very much. Many years went by, then at last, one day, a baby girl arrived.

'This is the happiest day of my life!' said the king. 'We will have a big christening and we will invite all the fairies!'

So the king and queen wrote to the yellow fairy, the orange fairy, the green fairy, the red fairy, the blue fairy, the pink fairy, and the little white fairy. But they didn't write to the black fairy, old Carabosse.

Carabosse was a bad fairy. She knew about the baby princess and the christening, so she came to the church. And when she saw all the other fairies there, she was very angry.

'Why didn't the king and queen invite me to the christening?' she said.

After the christening, they had
dinner. Everybody had gold cups
and gold plates.

When the queen saw Carabosse she said,
'Oh dear! Why didn't we invite her to the
christening?' She smiled at Carabosse, and said,
'I am very sorry. Please sit down with us now
and have dinner.'

The king told his servants, 'Bring another chair,
another cup, and another plate.'

But there were no more gold cups and plates, so
the servants gave Carabosse a silver cup and a
silver plate.

'What?' said Carabosse. 'No gold for me?'

After that, she was more angry.

After dinner, the fairies gave their presents to
the baby princess. The fairies' presents were
magic presents.

'The princess will be happy,' said the yellow fairy.

'And strong,' said the orange fairy.

'She will be beautiful,' said the blue fairy.

'And kind,' said the green fairy.

The red fairy said, 'She will have many friends.'

But the little white fairy didn't say anything.
She looked at Carabosse.

'Old Carabosse is going to say something nasty,'
she thought. 'I must speak after her. Then
perhaps I can do some good.' So the little white
fairy hid behind a curtain.

Then Carabosse slowly stood up.

'One day, this little princess will prick her finger on a spindle … and she will die!'

'NO!' said the king. 'Don't say that!'

'Please!' said the queen. 'She is our only child!'

Everybody in the room was afraid. They were all very quiet.

And then the little white fairy came out from behind the curtain.

'The princess will not die,' she said. 'She will only sleep. She will sleep for a hundred years. Then a prince will come and find her, and she will open her eyes again and be happy.'

6

'NO!' said the king again. 'It's not true. The princess will not prick her finger on a spindle, because there will not be any spindles.'

He told his servants, 'Go and find all the spinning wheels in the country. Look in every house. Bring them here.'

So his servants went to every house in the country and brought all the spinning wheels back to the castle. Then they made a big fire and burned them.

But they didn't find all of them. There was one old spinning wheel in a room in an old tower. But no one knew about it, so no one went and looked for it.

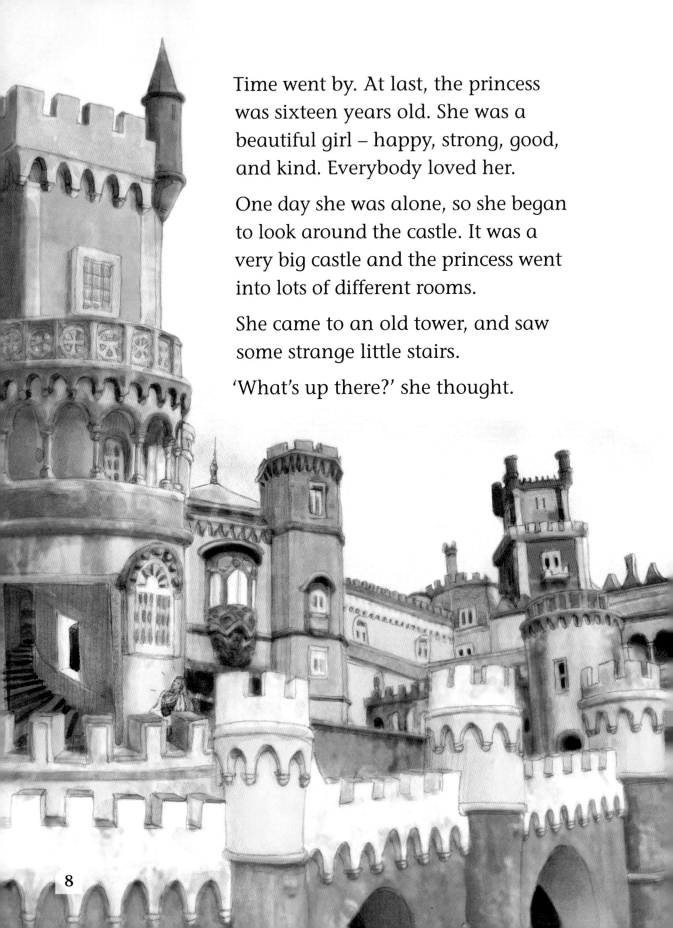

Time went by. At last, the princess was sixteen years old. She was a beautiful girl – happy, strong, good, and kind. Everybody loved her.

One day she was alone, so she began to look around the castle. It was a very big castle and the princess went into lots of different rooms.

She came to an old tower, and saw some strange little stairs.

'What's up there?' she thought.

Slowly the young princess went up the stairs.
Then she came to a door. She opened it, and
saw a little old woman and a strange wheel.

'Hello,' said the princess. 'What are you doing?
And what is that strange wheel?'

'It's a spinning wheel, my dear,' answered the
old woman. 'Would you like to see it? Come
closer and look ...'

'Here,' said the old woman, 'sit in my chair.'

'Thank you,' said the princess. 'You are very kind.'

She sat down and looked at the spinning wheel. Then she touched the spindle.

'Oh! It pricked me! It pricked my finger!'

'Oh dear!' said the old woman. 'Are you all right?'

But the princess didn't answer. She only fell quietly from her chair onto the floor.

'Oh dear! Oh dear!' said the old woman. 'What's wrong? I must go and get help.'

When the king heard, he was very angry. 'I don't understand. I said *Burn all the spinning wheels.*'

'Oh dear!' said the old woman. 'No one told me. My little room is in an old tower, far away from everybody.'

'We must find the little white fairy,' said the queen. 'She will help us.'

Then the king and queen put the princess on a gold bed. And they sat and watched her quietly, and waited for the little white fairy.

When the little white fairy heard about the princess, she flew through the sky in her magic coach. She arrived at the castle and ran to the king and queen.

'Do not cry and do not be afraid,' she told them. 'The princess is only sleeping. She will sleep quietly for a hundred years.'

Then the little white fairy said some magic words and everyone in the castle went to sleep: the king and queen, the lords and ladies, and all the servants. Even the king's horses and the king's dogs.

'You must all sleep for a hundred years,' said the little white fairy. 'Then the princess will not be alone when she opens her eyes again.'

The little white fairy walked through the castle. It was all quiet now. Then she went out and closed the big door quietly behind her.

And the princess and all the people in the castle slept. Tall trees and grass came up all around the castle, so no one could see it.

For many years no one visited the castle. Then one day, after a hundred years, a young prince came with his friends.

The prince saw the forest of tall trees, but he also saw the towers of the castle, far away. There was an old man on the road by the forest.

'What are those towers in the forest?' asked the prince. 'Is it a castle?'

'Yes,' said the old man, 'but no one goes there. Some people say that it's a witch's castle. But others say that a beautiful princess sleeps there, on a gold bed.'

'A princess!' said the prince. 'On a gold bed! I want to go up there and see.'

'But you can't go through the forest,' said the old man.

'Oh yes, I can!' said the prince.

The old man watched and the prince went up the hill on his white horse. Then a strange thing happened. The trees began to open, and the prince and his horse went through easily.

But the trees closed behind him, and his friends could not go after him.

So the prince went on alone and found the castle.

'This is a strange castle,' he said. 'Everybody is sleeping. And they are all wearing strange clothes. People wore clothes like these a hundred years ago.'

'Hello!' he called.

But nobody answered.

He was a little afraid and wanted to leave. But then he thought about the princess on her gold bed.

He looked for her, but he couldn't find her.
Then at last, upstairs, he opened an old door –
and there she was!

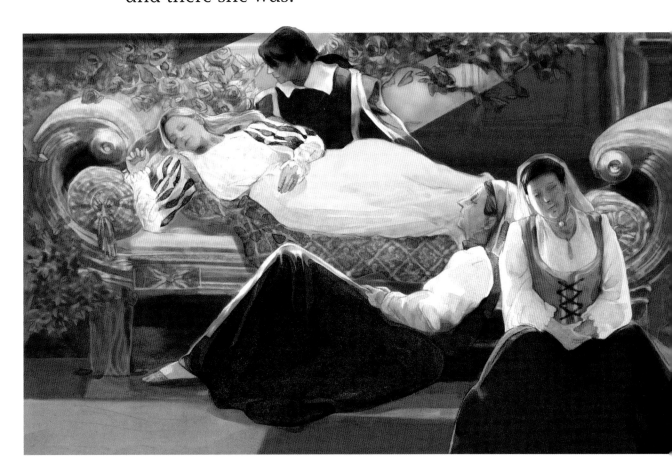

She slept on a gold bed. Her hair was long and
it was the colour of gold. The sun came through
the window and fell onto her face.

'Oh!' said the prince. 'She is very beautiful!'

He looked at her for a long, long time. Then
he put his hand on her hand and kissed her.

Suddenly she opened her eyes.

And when the princess opened her eyes, all the other people in the room began to open their eyes too.

'Will you marry me?' asked the prince.

'Oh yes!' said the princess. 'But first, I must eat something. I'm very hungry!'

'Let's go down then,' said the prince. 'Let's all go downstairs. There is food on the tables – and it's warm!'

One by one, everyone in the castle opened their eyes: the king and queen, the lords and ladies, and all the servants. Even the king's horses and the king's dogs.

Later that day the prince and the princess went to the church, and they were married.

Outside the castle it was summer. The grass was green, the sky was blue, and all the birds sang.

And so the years went by. The prince and princess had two children: a little girl with gold hair, like her mother, and a little boy with dark hair, like his father.

And they all lived happily ever after.

1 Write the words and find the name of somebody in the story.

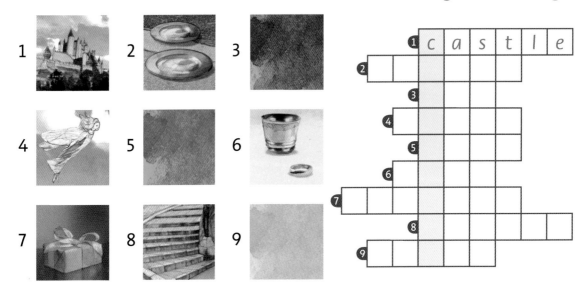

2 Find the page and answer the questions.

1 Why did the servants give Carabosse a silver cup and plate?
page 4   _Because there were no more gold cups and plates._

2 What did the king's servants do to the spinning wheels they found?

_____   _____

3 Where did the king and queen put the princess after she pricked her finger?

_____   _____

4 How did the little white fairy make everyone in the castle go to sleep?

_____   _____

5 What happened when the prince kissed the princess?

_____   _____

3 Who is speaking? Write the name for 1–4.
For number 5, what does the queen say? Write one sentence.

1 'Why didn't the king and queen invite me to the christening?'
   Carabosse
2 'Find all the spinning wheels in the country. Bring them here.'

   _____
3 'It pricked me! It pricked my finger!'   _____
4 'This is a strange castle. Everybody is sleeping.'   _____
5 _____   _the queen_

4 Complete the sentences with the past tense of these verbs.

come up   ~~be~~   close   can   sleep   go

It ___was___ all quiet in the castle now. The little white fairy _____ out and _____ the big door quietly behind her.

And the princess and all the people in the castle _____ for a hundred years. No one _____ see the castle because tall trees and grass _____ all around it.

21

Glossary

alone not with other people

burned past tense of **burn**: to put something in a fire

castle

christening when a baby gets his / her name, in a church

church a building where people go to pray

coach

cups

curtain

fairy

fire

flew past tense of **fly**: to go through the air

floor
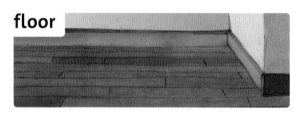

food things that people or animals eat

forest a place with many trees

gold *a gold ring*

grass

hid past tense of **hide**: to go where no one can see you

invite to ask someone to come

kissed past tense of **kiss**

lords and ladies rich and important men and women

marry to become someone's husband or wife

plates

present

prick

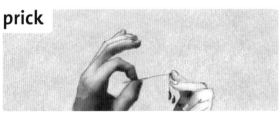

prince a king or queen's son

princess a king or queen's daughter

servant a person who works in someone's house and cooks or cleans

silver *silver cups*

spindle part of a spinning wheel

spinning wheel

stairs

tower

Classic Tales

Classic stories retold for learners of English – bringing the magic of traditional storytelling to the language classroom

Level 1: 100 headwords
- The Enormous Turnip
- The Little Red Hen
- Lownu Mends the Sky
- The Magic Cooking Pot
- Mansour and the Donkey
- Peach Boy
- The Princess and the Pea
- Rumpelstiltskin
- The Shoemaker and the Elves
- Three Billy-Goats

Level 2: 150 headwords
- Amrita and the Trees
- Big Baby Finn
- The Fisherman and his Wife
- The Gingerbread Man
- Jack and the Beanstalk
- Thumbelina
- The Town Mouse and the Country Mouse
- The Ugly Duckling

Level 3: 200 headwords
- Aladdin
- Goldilocks and the Three Bears
- The Little Mermaid
- Little Red Riding Hood

Level 4: 300 headwords
- Cinderella
- The Goose Girl
- Sleeping Beauty
- The Twelve Dancing Princesses

Level 5: 400 headwords
- Beauty and the Beast
- The Magic Brocade
- Pinocchio
- Snow White and the Seven Dwarfs

All *Classic Tales* have an accompanying
- **e-Book with Audio Pack** containing the book and the e-book with audio, for use on a computer or CD player. Teachers can also project the e-book onto an interactive whiteboard to use it like a Big Book.
- **Activity Book and Play** providing extra language practice and the story adapted as a play for performance in class or on stage.

For more details, visit
www.oup.com/elt/readers/classictales

OXFORD
UNIVERSITY PRESS

Great Clarendon Street, Oxford OX2 6DP

Oxford University Press is a department of the University of Oxford. It furthers the University's objective of excellence in research, scholarship, and education by publishing worldwide in

Oxford New York

Auckland Cape Town Dar es Salaam Hong Kong Karachi Kuala Lumpur Madrid Melbourne Mexico City Nairobi New Delhi Shanghai Taipei Toronto

With offices in

Argentina Austria Brazil Chile Czech Republic France Greece Guatemala Hungary Italy Japan Poland Portugal Singapore South Korea Switzerland Thailand Turkey Ukraine Vietnam

OXFORD and OXFORD ENGLISH are registered trade marks of Oxford University Press in the UK and in certain other countries

ISBN: 978 0 19 423954 7

This *Classic Tale* title is available as an e-Book with Audio Pack
ISBN: 978 0 19 423957 8

Also available: Sleeping Beauty Activity Book and Play
ISBN: 978 0 19 423955 4

Printed in China

This book is printed on paper from certified and well-managed sources.

ACKNOWLEDGEMENTS

Illustrated by: Jérôme Brasseur / Beehive Illustration